The Man in the Van

by Jeff Novotny
Illustrated by Makoto Okada

Staten House

Copyright ©2024 by Jeff Novotny

All rights reserved.

ISBN: 979-8-89379-394-9 (E-book)
        979-8-89379-392-5 (hardcover)

Printed in the United States of America

First printing 2024

Preface note:

The reader is assured that no children were misgendered in the writing of this book. Because that's literally figuratively the worst thing you can do to a child. Much worse than...well, you'll see....

'Twas a beautiful daybreak, the sun shining in,
A lovelier morning there never had been.

Bright sunbeams a-dancing in this cheerful room,
Where a curious figure stood wielding a broom.

Sweeping the floor and toiling away,
As this was to be a most special day.

He looked out the window and gazed at the sun,
Inviting him out for lascivious fun.

A familiar feeling coursed through his veins,
A peculiar want which seemed never to wane;

The gnawing obsession pervading his mind,
All his best efforts in vain to unwind.

This was a chap who made it his mission
To frolic with youngsters, in every position.

Though he chronically longed to cavort with a child,
Let's not use the moniker ending with "-phile."

Instead, witness a man, a van, and a plan:
This is the tale of a fellow named Stan.

Quite tired of reading of things he would do,
Today was the day he'd make them come true.*

---

* To his dismay, Stan hadn't been on a playdate in a while. The last one went something like this:
Stan: It's nice to meet you.
Young Companion: The pleasure is mine.
Stan: Um, no, it's mine.
Companion: It's mine, give it back!
Stan: Stop it!
Companion: Mom!

But first it was time to get stylishly dressed;
It's always important to be at your best.

As he glued on his mustache and bushy eyebrows,
He was sure the police wouldn't recognize him now.

Stan had to take great care not to be seen –
To be caught meant a minimum ten to fifteen,

And the last time he ended up in the can
He became the "girlfriend" of a very large man.

So with a good breakfast, and a glance at his phone,
He was sure he would not spend tonight all alone.

He remembered the places where he couldn't go,
As he got into mischief there not long ago.

And now, to ensure the success of his plan:
A quick buff and shine of his spiffy white van.

It was the only thing he'd kept in the divorce
...and the restraining order, of course.*

---

* Since his divorce, Stan had lived in some of the ~~nicest~~ places in town: Crackview Gardens, Guttervale, Dumpton Springs, d'Éprivation, Project 420, and Stabbington.

His loyal companion, his chariot, conspired;
Together the two would pursue his desires.

Starting it up, it sputtered alive,
Just like it did back in old '85.

Bouncing along in his trusty machine,
He took in the picturesque neighborhood scene.

At the corner he came upon jolly Mr. Chen,
Who greeted him with,

"I tell you last time, no come back here again!"

Like a siren, the road beckoned urgently on,
"Quickly now, Stan, or your chance will be gone."

At 10 o'clock sharp the patrolman would come,
Which surely would spell an end to his fun.

In no time, he arrived at a bustling playground
With frolicking kids, and no grown-ups around.

Lurking in shadows behind the tall weeds,
He knew this was the place to fulfill his Needs.

There were youngsters and fledglings, children and kids –
One of these soon would surely be his.

A banquet of youth, a buffet of spawn,
A statutory inventory pranced on the lawn.

Rugrats, moppets, sprouts, tots, and tykes,
An enticing young menu, riding on bikes.

Juveniles, underage, minors, jailbait –
Mouth watering now, he scarcely could wait….

But which to select? A true Sophi(l)e's Choice,
Culling just one of these tasty young boys

Was like choosing his favorite fungal disease
Or putting lipstick on his headless Barbies.*

---

* The fashionable new Disabled Minority Trans-Cowboy Barbie™

But one specimen played with particular glee –
This was the one he'd collect secretly.

He slithered right over surreptitiously
And called forth the "player" he knew he could be.

"Well hello, little man, what's your name?"
Polished and suave, at the top of his game.

"I'm Kaysen," said the bubbly tot with a grin.
"You mean Jason?" Stan asked, scratching his chin.

"No, my folks were too hip to write it that way;
Their spell-checker must've been broken that day."

With this kind of name it was utterly clear:
Hipster parents trying to out-cool their old peers.

They'd chosen a name that was tricky to spell
So he'd be unique, just like everyone else.*

---

* Note to parents: to come up with a hip, postmodern name for your child that shows how sophisticated you think you are, just take a normal name and start replacing the letters until it looks sufficiently odd. Xe will have a pretentious-sounding name for xyrself in no time!

Stan thought of a ruse, a gambit, a ploy
Which surely would work on this tender young boy.

"Could you help me find my poor lost cat?
I've looked all around and can't see where he's at.

He must be afraid, and lonely too,
Which is why I will need some help from you."

Kaysen wanted to help, but he wasn't quite sure –
Somehow he'd heard this story before…

But a scavenger hunt would be marvelous fun!
He'd pet the lil' kitty, and pet him a ton.*

"And I've got a van you wouldn't believe –
When kids come to see it, sometimes they don't leave.

When we get there you'll meet other boys too,
All of them anxiously waiting for you:†

Aiden, Brayden, Hayden, and Jayden,
Kayden, Ja'Kwayden, Sprayden, al-Qaiden,
Harper, Jaxson, Lincoln,‡ and Ames;
Their parents come up with the trendiest names
To make them unique – now they all sound the same.

An assembly of kiddos whom you'll just adore…
And now the best part: I have candy galore!"

Kaysen liked candy!

---

* Of course, Stan didn't really have a cat. But he did have an emotional-support tapeworm named Clyde. Clyde's favorite foods were undercooked poultry and shellfish.
† Stan had lots of (very) young friends because he ~~snatched~~ met people wherever he went.
‡ *Parents: do NOT name your child this.*

"My favorite flavor is cherry," he beamed.*
"Mine too," tittered Stan, with a devilish gleam.

Stan opened his coat, exposing his stash;
This maneuver unfailingly landed his catch.

---

* Kaysen once found some little blue candy pills in his daddy's bathroom, so he asked what flavor they were. And his daddy said they were the bitter taste of disappointment. That did not sound yummy. "And who is this pool-cleaning guy who keeps showing up every time I go out of town?" asked his daddy. Kaysen remembered that his name was Manuel.

"First on the menu are letters today:
GHB, LSD, MDMA,
Vitamin G, TNT, and Special K."

Kaysen was glad he'd learned his ABC's
But he'd never heard of treats such as these.

Try out the girls and you'll feel rather zippy:
There's Oxy and Roxy and Molly and Skippy,
Addy, Miss Emma, Kloreen, Arsenicki.

And let's not forget all the fun things to sniff:
There's Gloo, Deezle, Wipkreem, and Squiff,
Gas-O-Leen, Whippets, Poppers, and Spliff.

But wait, there's much more, it doesn't stop there –
The wackiest names of which I'm aware:

Fizzies, Benzeeni, Queevils, and Tranks,
Zannies and Roofies and P-Funk and Quanks.

And the king of them all (or maybe the queen):
Trans-2-(1H-indol-3-yl)-1-methyl-ethylamine!"

So many choices! The boy stopped in his tracks,
Tempted by visions of sugary snacks.

The candy was strange, he had to admit,
But trying new things didn't scare him one bit.

Cautious, he warned, "But my mom always said,
Don't talk to strangers – go and find her instead."*

"But surely you see, lad, your mother's not here,
And I can assure you, you've nothing to fear."

His Mom was at home, and his Daddy away –
The pool-cleaning man was visiting that day.†

"We've no time to spare – kitty needs to be found.
So come on and let's have a good look around."

———————————

* Although Stan was most likely not this boy's mother, so many children called him Daddy that he often forgot which one was his real Daddy.
† And they didn't even have a pool! His mother said this little arrangement was due to his daddy's "performance issues" so she was "pursuing alternative sources." It sure sounded complicated! And his mother assured him that yes, it was very complicated.

Excitedly, Kaysen took the man's hand;
Stan led him away, to do as he'd planned.

And there in the shadows, parked slightly askew,
Was Stan's noble steed, nearly hidden from view.

"At last, here we are!" our man said with pride.
"Come on, let's go see what's waiting inside."

But Kaysen sensed something suspicious here:
The van's registration had expired last year.

But he wanted the goodies, and offered a plea:
"But Stan, you said there was candy for me."

Stan knew he would have to ease the boy's mind,
So he called on a trick which would keep him in line.

Now for the closer, sealing the deal –
So giddy and eager he felt he could squeal.

"You see, there's something I want you to do,
But after we're finished, there's candy for you.

In less than two minutes I'll surely be done –
That's why my ex-wife says I'm no fun."

For Kaysen this was nothing new;
His Uncle Melvin made him do…certain things, too.

Stan opened the door – it was quite dark inside.
But it was too late – there was nowhere to hide.

Stan led the boy in with glee and delight;
With a devious grin, he turned on the light.

As Kaysen peered in, just what did he see?

A beautiful scene of Diversity!

Behold, in the van was a dazzling sight,
Kids of all shapes and colors, and not too many White.

The ideal percentage and number of each,
A perfect reflection of society's reach.

Equality ruled – there were most every kind;
Clearly no child had been left behind.

Standing before them and teeming with pride,
Stan nobly addressed those his pursuit had supplied:

"How do we welcome our new friend today?
What are we always required to say?"

What our hero had learned by watching the news –
You must always affirm the compulsory view:

Diversequinclusity must be the way,
The law of the land in this enlightened day

If the faces around you look too much alike,
You've done it all wrong, so now make it right;

Surround yourself with a colorful crowd,
Then whatever you do, you can truly be proud.

Hearing this message, Stan knew it was true,
And so it was clear just what he had to do:

He'd vary his harvest, year after year,
To check all the boxes and live without fear.

He'd assembled a rainbow, a palette of hues,
A many-faced prism of children to use.

He'd woven a patchwork of sizes and tones
Who'd make him feel special, and never alone.
(and weight for the rear wheels, for traction in snow)

"There's a place just for you, next to Ellison here;
He's been my companion for more than two years.

He doesn't talk much, except when he's bad;
Then we correct him.
"Hmphphfnmphfnm," choked the lad.*

---

* Stan could only hope that Ellison hadn't once again fouled his water dish.

Turning to Kaysen with ravenous eyes,
He'd finally savor his succulent prize.

Now that his prey was within easy reach,
He'd tear right into this juicy lil' peach.

But suddenly, his phone began to sound…
He quickly made sure there was no one around.

You see, Stan was quite a popular guy
Upon whom the community could rely.

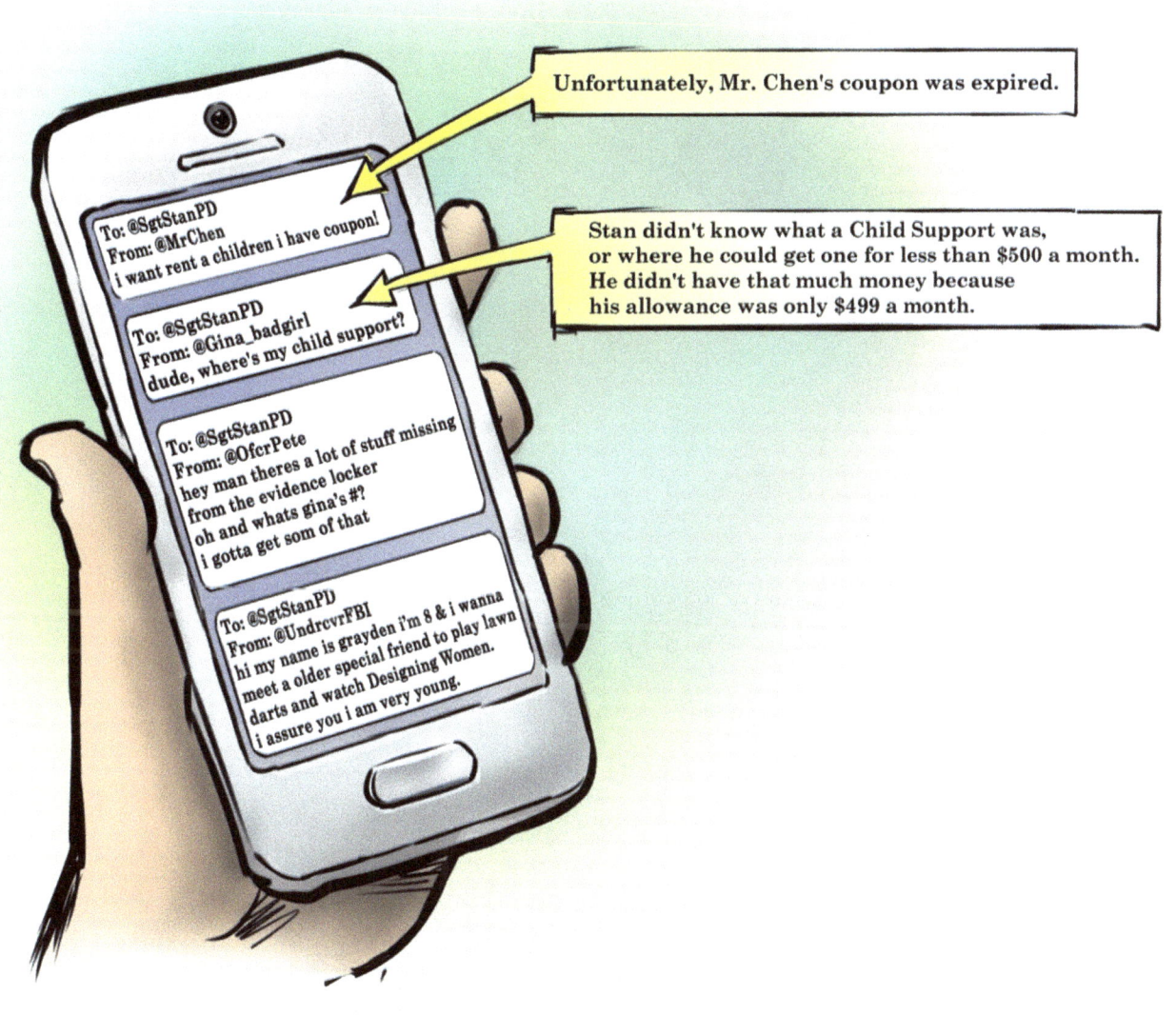

So what happened next, what came to pass,
As our hero captured his quarry at last?

We can't watch the fun that took place in the van,
As keeping it secret is part of the plan.

But as Stan enjoyed what he'd hotly desired,
His ethnicity quotas were met as required.

So now a brief lesson, as in tales such as this,
We mustn't forget, we mustn't dismiss.

Some strangers are good, and some not so much;
If you're "underrepresented" as such

You too could garner a coveted spot
In the quest to collect cosmopolitan tots.

Liams and Carters and Addisons too –
Stan and his gang want to party with you.

Kids grow up so fast in the back of a van
As they quickly find out what their ~~captor~~ playmate has planned.

A promise of puppies, surprises, and more –
You never know what's behind the van door.

But always remember, for better or worse:
If you go with a stranger, GET THE CANDY FIRST!

www.ingramcontent.com/pod-product-compliance
Lightning Source LLC
Chambersburg PA
CBHW061358010526
44107CB00012B/979